slow miracles

slow miracles

urban women fighting for liberation

by G. F. Thompson

LuraMedia™

LuraMedia, Inc.
7060 Miramar Road, #104
San Diego, CA 92121

Library of Congress Cataloging-in-Publication Data
Thompson, G.F., date.
    Slow miracles : urban women fighting for liberation /
    by G.F. Thompson.
        p.   cm.
    ISBN 1-880913-12-7
    1. Urban women—United States—Social conditions—Case studies.
    2. Working class women—United States—Social conditions—Case
    studies. 3. Women's rights—United States—Case studies.
    I. Title.
    HQ1426.T54   1995   94-43246
    305.42'0973—dc20   CIP

To my husband,
who believes
that the voices of the women in this book
should be heard,
and who shows it
in a remarkably practical way
by taking care of kids, animals, doorbells,
dirty dishes, bill collectors, and everything else
each time I sit down to write.

And, with love and gratitude,
to the women of Joint Ministry Project
and the women of First Church.

CONTENTS

PROLOGUE

BIRTHING MOSES

Exodus 1:13-2:11 (New Revised Standard Version)

The Egyptians became ruthless in imposing tasks on the Israelites, and made their lives bitter with hard service in mortar and brick and in every kind of field labor. They were ruthless in all the tasks that they imposed on them.

The king of Egypt said to the Hebrew midwives, one of whom was named Shiphrah and the other Puah, "When you act as midwives to the Hebrew women, and see them on the birthstool, if it is a boy, kill him; but if it is a girl, she shall live."

But the midwives feared God; they did not do as the king of Egypt commanded them, but let the boys live.

So the king of Egypt summoned the midwives, and said to them, "Why have you done this, and allowed the boys to live?"

The midwives said to Pharaoh, "Because the Hebrew women are not like the Egyptian women; for they are vigorous and give birth before the midwife comes to them."

So God dealt well with the midwives, and the people multiplied and became very strong. And because the midwives feared God, he gave them families.

Then Pharaoh commanded all his people, "Every boy that is born to the Hebrews, you shall throw into the Nile, but you shall let every girl live."

Now a man from the house of Levi went and married a Levite woman. The woman conceived and bore a son; and when she saw he was a fine baby, she hid him for three months. When she could hide him no longer, she got a papyrus basket for him, and plastered it with bitumen and pitch; and she put the child in it and placed it among the reeds in the bank of the river. His sister stood at a distance, to see what would happen to him.

The daughter of Pharaoh came down to bathe at the river, while her attendants walked beside the river. She saw the basket among the reeds and sent her maid to bring it. When she opened it, she saw the child. He was crying, and she took pity on him. "This must be one of the Hebrew's children," she said.

Then his sister said to Pharaoh's daughter, "Shall I go and get you a nurse from the Hebrew women to nurse the child for you?"

Pharaoh's daughter said to her, "Yes."

So the girl went and called the child's mother. Pharaoh's daughter said to her, "Take this child and nurse it for me, and I will give you your wages."

So the woman took the child and nursed it. When the child grew up, she brought him to Pharaoh's daughter, and she took him as her son. She named him Moses, "because," she said, "I drew him out of the water."

* * *

This passage ushers us into one of the most revolutionary texts of our times, the Moses story. Within the riveting symbology of that story − the burning bush, the splitting sea, the endless stretch of wilderness and its surprise of manna, the yearned-for land of milk and honey − marginalized peoples across the world are able to gather fresh momentum and power.

It serves as a guide to many, from theologians to grassroots organizers to third-world base communities.

Deeply embedded in the Moses story is the metaphor of battle. Pharaoh is an evil force whose defeat requires organization of power, determination on the part of the people, and a flight to freedom. Justice, unevenly distributed, must be claimed in God's holy name. The story comes complete with weapons, chariots, rivers of blood, and warriors drowned − all the accouterments of war.

This story of victory over Pharaoh has held me together upon more than one occasion. As an ordained woman whose ministry has been formed largely in the urban core, I have seen that Pharaoh wears many hats in the city: economic disparity, bureaucracy, war trauma, mental illness, chemical addiction, hopelessness, substandard housing, child abuse and neglect, rape, chaos, starvation, crime, and premature death. Without this vision of victory over Pharaoh, without some clue that the plagues can be weathered, I would have given up long ago. How often have I wondered, Now, isn't it time, God, for the sea to split? Or, Praise God, Manna! And right out of a dumpster!

In my own heart the word Moses is synonymous with the word liberation. And liberation so often requires a fight. A fight with Pharaoh.

And yet, and yet . . . if the word Moses is indeed synonymous with the word liberation, then one might rightly wonder, particularly at times when the battle seems a losing one, about the birth of Moses: the point in time before which liberation had virtually no existence in our faith history; the point after which liberation came into possibility. The birth point of freedom from oppression. A place to look for some sign of hope.

I have focused often in recent months upon this birthing moment and have found no warriors, no masses of brave armored marchers, no signs of war. Instead, I have found a little clump of women: two old midwives, a young slave mother who will not give in, her brave daughter, the daughter of Pharaoh himself, and her attendant.

Pharaoh had made himself very clear: He wanted the baby Moses dead. Wanted all the Hebrew man-children dead. Wanted all hope of liberation strangled at the birthing stool. It was this odd collection of women, who did not know one another and had no public power whatsoever, who managed to keep Moses alive. Managed to keep him alive, despite their various burdens of patriarchy and slavery. They would not let that baby die.

Liberation may be looked upon as a war, but the presence of these women in the Moses story hints that it could also be looked upon as a birth — a birth of hope. Those engaged in its process could be called warriors. They might also be called midwives. These women had no weapons but their own craftiness, their own faith in one another and in God, their own deepest desire that life win over death. They would have been killed in any kind of external battle. The war metaphor could not really sustain them, in the end. Only the birth metaphor could. And so it did.

Some see war and birth as opposites, the one dealing death and the other rendering life. I would disagree. It is not that simple. In important ways birth is akin to sheer revolution. It is a ripping forth of the new from the old. It is bloody and excruciating, close to the cusp of life and death.

The story of Moses' victory could not exist without the

preceding story of Moses' birth. So take note, Pharaoh. Take hope, Israelites. Take hope, those with too little food and shelter and too few jobs and too much abuse or alienation for any human heart to bear. Take hope, those whose weapons have been stripped. It may well be that what the warriors have not been able to accomplish, the midwives will.

My ministry has led me, blessedly, to those who birth Moses day after day. I have seen them and come to know them while they labor in their churches, in their streets, and in their homes. Women of different ages and classes and races and religions, just like their biblical mothers.

Although lacking the weaponry of public status, these women understand their connected diversity to be a great source of power and a gift from God. They have earned my deep respect, for their intent is to give birth to liberation, again and again. They want it alive. And that is just how they bring it forth: tiny, perhaps, but screaming and full of spunk; starving hungry, perhaps, and bloodied, but capable of miraculous growth, eager for a teat. Liberation.

In the pages of this book, I am honored to bring them to you: once Shiphrah, Puah, Miriam; now Lydia, Helen, Tami, Nadine, and all the others. The one I speak of most, though, is the one borne of my own fragmented longings and hopes. I call her, and in my heart know her to be, "Pharaoh's Daughter."

CHAPTER 1
PHARAOH'S DAUGHTER

The old black dog never disobeys. Meek, he never even glances up, but lies still, eyes closed, tail tucked under. If I become curious about some part of him — the glassy deep brown of his eye, or his teeth or his paws — I simply look. Pull up a lid or a lip with the sticky, untender hands of a pre-schooler. And the old black dog licks me then, as though I taste good, like buttered toast or bananas — the things I love to eat.

The old black dog always minds. So that when my father says, "Sit," he sits. When my father says, "Kennel," he limps out the door to the fenced backyard. Too old to move fast, he always makes it clear that he is moving in the right direction, if slowly.

On this winter morning, the old black dog lies by the kitchen door as usual. My mother has come down and thrown open the drapes, put the coffee water on. I am sitting on the stool by the stove to watch her cook. When my father strides in, all in khaki — weekend clothes — he does what he has always done: opens the door and says, "Kennel," to the old black dog.

This time, the old black dog just lies there. His eyes do not open, though his tail thumps ever so slightly. My father says, "Kennel," a little louder, and louder again. The sound coming into his throat frightens me. Louder still. His face is becoming a deep, angry red. "Kennel! Kennel! Kennel, you stupid animal!"

The old black dog does not look up, does not move. He just lies there. I wonder if he is dying, or dead, or just — finally — bold. All at once my father, spitting with rage, jerks off his belt and begins thrashing the old black dog, shouting, "Kennel," with every stroke. "Kennel, I said Kennel!"

I feel sick. My mother picks me up quickly, carries me into the other room. We sit on the edge of the couch, my mother and I, listening to the sounds of the belt lash, my father's screams, then the slam of the back door, the starting up of the station wagon, the screech of wheels down the drive.

When we tiptoe back into the silence of the kitchen, the old black dog is gone. And when my father returns a few hours later, he mutters, "He's gone, he's dead." There are tear-stains on his splotchy face.

All at once, inside of me, there is grief, rage, confusion. The old black dog, the old black dog, the gentle old black dog. Why, why, but why?

I believe I can hold it in, so long as my father doesn't touch me. If he just stays away from me. If I can just escape his skin. I avert my eyes, I become all still. Don't touch me, don't touch me . . .

But he does touch me.

He comes to me, and puts his arms around me, and speaks strange words about what happened, words that roar crazy in my head. Too much, too much, the warmth of his flesh. All I can do, all I can even try to do, is close my eyes and hold on, don't move, don't fight, hold the hurt inside, where it will not get me in trouble, hold still, hold still, hold still . . .

And so it is that I learn what it has really been like. To be the old black dog, that is.

CHAPTER 2
LYDIA

She was sick of the cockroaches, who wouldn't be? So were the other women sick of the cockroaches, all the units had them. The landlord, where was he? He lived somewhere else. "Put out boric acid," he said. "Nothing I can do."

The cockroaches, virulent, began to win. The children would open a cereal box and . . . Pop! Out jumped a cockroach. Pick up a dishrag, out slithered a cockroach. Cockroaches in the cupboards, in the sheets, in the tub of margarine, between the plates. Big ones, big enough to scare the littler kids not accustomed to them yet. Big, shiny, evil cockroaches. Everywhere.

She knew, Lydia did, that there were health regulations. But the angry Chicana flash of her voice seemed to make people ignore her on the phone, so that the health officials, like the landlord, would refer her to another number or tell her in a bored tone of voice about this solution or that. And all the while, the cockroaches were multiplying. Destroying the food her children needed to eat. She would take off her shoe and smash them in a crashing rage. Just as brazen, they kept coming.

The idea came to her in the night. She spoke with the women in the other units. They loved it.

When morning came, one woman took the biggest cockroach she could find to her temporary secretarial job and stuck it on the copy machine, where she blew the image up big and made many copies.

Another woman wrote out the press release:

COCKROACHES TO PROTEST
AT LANDLORD'S PRIVATE HOME.

It featured a story about cockroaches at a certain inner-city address who had become so sick of humans interfering with their lives that they organized a march and a protest rally to take place at the landlord's lovely suburban home. The date and location were identified.

Lydia herself attached the huge copies of the cock-roaches to the press releases and sent the mailings. She didn't need to do follow-up calls. The press contacted her.

The children had an important job: catching cock-roaches. Their mothers set up a contest — a penny a roach, with a bonus for the highest count. It kept them busy all Saturday, slamming the lids on jelly jars and mason jars and kitchen pots. In excited groups they combed the building. Even the littlest ones. By evening, thousands of roaches were ready to march.

One woman had located a van. Into this, the mothers and their children and their roaches climbed the following morning. The drive to the landlord's home was lengthy, deep to the heart of an outer suburb, where none of them had ever been before.

The TV cameras met them at his address. The roaches, crushed on top of one another and packed too tightly by little hands, were eager to escape, ready to march. Lydia had the children line them up in their containers across the front lawn, a child standing at each one, ready to release the roaches. She gave her interview, telling of conditions in the rental units, telling of the lack of cooperation from any official source, telling of the roach-infested food that her children needed.

Then she told the children, "When I say 'Ready, Set, GO,' you lift the lids and let the roaches have their march, okay?"

The children were excited. They were ready. The TV cameras zoomed in.

"Ready, Set . . . "

Oh, here comes the landlord! He wants to set things straight! He will fumigate the building. He will save the children. He will, he will, he will . . .

But the children are too excited, too primed, too ready to spill filthy cockroaches all over this neatly mown, emerald-green lawn in this neighborhood that has no broken glass in the streets and no windows boarded up and no scary people on the corner. "Hooray!" they shout, and all the lids come off at once, for Lydia has lost control of them − or so it would seem to an untrained eye − and they fling roaches in every direction. It is raining, raining cockroaches in the suburbs, on TV. A plague on Pharaoh all over again, this time in living color.

The units in Lydia's building don't have cockroaches anymore.

CHAPTER 3
PHARAOH'S DAUGHTER

The only thing surely right is my nighty, for it is my favorite. It flows to the floor in a certain way that makes me feel a little bit like a princess, or perhaps even a queen, though I am only five.

The rest is not right. The room is dark, the door shut. There seems to be at least one witch under the bed. Also, they are fighting, my mother and father, I do not know why. Fighting downstairs and behind closed doors, so that crashes and curses and scary sounds come to me muffled through the walls. I am cold.

I try quietly, oh so quietly, to go find my sister, my long-yellow-haired big sister who loves me. I tiptoe down the hall toward her room. But he hears me somehow, hears the hinge squeak on my bedroom door, or perhaps the floor boards moving. Screams at me to stay in there, get back in my bed right now.

The bathroom stands between myself and the journey back. Anything, anything but the pitch black of my own room, my own terrifying bed, the witches, the sounds past the walls.

The bathroom at least is bright and white. I stand in the middle of it, sucking in air, swirling my nighty. Then I climb up onto the white sink, grabbing hold of the polished faucet with a pretty mermaid on top, a mermaid cold and shiny. From there, I can reach the medicine cabinet.

Lovely red cough syrup, bright and clear, I drink it all. Then the baby aspirin, tiny pills that explode dry in my mouth, tart and pink. Then the green, is it mouthwash, so fiery on its way down? And then, and then, the blue and white tiles of the floor, the over-and-over blue flower patterns I have always loved, come crashing up to me in slow motion. Something else flies and crashes against the wall, and then finally, finally, everything in the world grows, blessedly, silent. Still as stone.

The lady has to keep saying it: "You're in the hospital, you're in the hospital, honey." Her skin is so beautiful, I stare and stare at it under the blinding white lights. Brown skin, smooth and soothing, like chocolate milk, except in the palms that skim over me, tucking in sheets, patting me tenderly. I have never seen brown skin before.

"What's your name?" I ask.

"My name's Olivia, baby. I'm your nurse."

She wears a bright white uniform and smells like talcum and bleach. She strokes my forehead.

She keeps speaking to me, in a soft voice that lilts and slants in ways unlike any I've ever known. "We had to pump your stomach, honey, and get all the medicine out. Your throat might be hurting you a little bit when you get home. Maybe your mama could bring you a dish of ice cream, baby. Everything is going to be all right now, it'll all be all right . . ."

She stays with me a for a long, long time, her gentleness washing over me like a dream.

And then the doctor comes in, pulling my eyelids this way and that, doing things with little lights and tongue depressors. Then he says that I can go home.

My princess nighty is ruined, covered with red stains. She sits me up on the hospital bed and slips it over my head anyway, for it is all I have. "Now I'll call for your mama, honey, I have to go."

Don't go . . .

She does go, though, she has to go. I have known all along she would have to. My mother comes in then, and takes me home, *and puts me back in my same bed with the witches under it, but it is quieter now, and I am tired.*

I don't know where my father has gone, but he is there again the next morning at the kitchen table, reading the paper.

CHAPTER 4
HELEN

If a powerful leader is recognizable by the number of people who trust her or him to protect their self-interests, then that woman who stays home days in a working neighborhood can become a very powerful leader indeed. Everybody's kid ends up in her care. Everybody's self-interest gets their nose wiped by her, gets their belly filled with her peanut butter and Saltines, gets their hair ruffled and their manners honed around her kitchen table. And no working, loving mother on the block is going to mess with her.

In fact, they'll protect her. They all need her. Desperately. She's on every school emergency record card. Her number is taped on every fridge. Every kid knows to turn to her in the long hollow hours when their own houses are empty.

Such a woman was Helen, in her younger days. She will tell you about it. How her yard bore a dirt-diamond scar every year by World Series time. How her front hall looked like a Lost-and-Found. How dollies from down the street, dollies with snarled hair, blinking eyelids stuck open, and cracked or missing limbs, would arrive most days for bread-and-water birthday parties, cradled and kissed in the arms of their pretending mothers.

She will tell you about it. How they were all white kids at first and then gradually became a mix of white and black and brown and yellow and red. They would fight sometimes. Nigger! Ofay! Spick! Gook! She would gather them round her then and inform them, icily, that if she were to peel their tender young skins off right then and there, they'd be identical underneath. So stop it. Now.

They listened to her. They craved what she had to offer. And after they grew up, they would come back and find her. She stayed put, Helen did. A person could come back and find her, it was one of her virtues. Come back and tell her about the harvests of the passing years: the diploma hard won, the marriage turned sour, the promotion, the stillbirth.

When her own children were grown and her husband dead, Helen kept on. She honed her skills on how to wrastle down politicians, corner this elected official or that, get what the neighborhood needed. She was good. Tough. Crafty. Persistent. A natural. And definitely, she was beloved, which gave her immense power.

Now Helen is older. They've brought in professional community organizers. Young men, mostly, who demand, demand, demand that people be on time, be there alert and ready to charge ahead, no excuses. No excuses for dozing off in your armchair and missing the start of a meeting, like she did the other night. No excuses. It's all about accountability to them, and numbers.

She knows what they think of her. Blue-haired little old lady. She knows.

But she's still the same old protectress of love and life that she always has been. She will not be put down. Getting put down is bad strategy, and anyway she's carrying too many souls of kinfolk and neighbors inside of her to risk the crash.

And so, she goes forth one last time. "Listen," she says to those young professional organizers, those young men who haven't really learned anything about life yet, "just because there's snow on my roof doesn't mean that my furnace is out! Timeliness is not the most important thing. And not numbers. And not accountability. No, no, no. Pay attention now. Treating each other right is the most important thing."

She says it again, even more firmly, looking them right in the eye. "Treating each other right. You know, or you oughta know. And so. I quit dealing with your be-on-time-or-else organization. As of now. Right now. Today, that is."

Helen. A woman of principle. A woman of dignity.

CHAPTER 5

PHARAOH'S DAUGHTER

My mother has tried and tried to get me out of it. "Green jumper, green jumper," she mutters. "Is that all you ever want to wear? Someday it will wear out on you, and then where will you be?"

Still, I wear the green jumper. Morning after morning.

Today, I have it on again. Bold temperas of happy houses gird the classroom walls. Janet Stein has just told Teacher that the rain outside sounds to her like millions of tiny horses prancing on the roof of school. For this, she gets a great deal of attention. The faces of the children are all pink, bobbing round me like clean pink helium balloons on strings. Buoyant, eager. I smell chalk dust, paste.

Now Teacher stands before us with alphabet cards. She holds up the D, and pink hands fly into the air. Some lucky, called-upon child sings out, "Dog!" or "Deer!" − it has to be an animal, that is the rule − and then Teacher goes on to E. Elephant. Fox. Giraffe.

Until we come to N.

The children are stumped. We are all thinking hard. I want to be like Janet Stein, to say the right thing and win the prize of Teacher's smile. Suddenly it comes to me, up shoots my hand, the only hand in class, reaching for the golden apple.

Teacher smiles. She calls on me − me, the one in the green jumper. And that is when I say it.

"Nigger! It's Nigger!"

All at once all the children are laughing, laughing so loud it roars. Teacher's forehead lines show anger, or is it sorrow, I can't tell, I can't tell. The laughter is so deafening it sears to the bone. I pound at my ears, squeeze my eyes shut, driven so far inside myself that even the green jumper is no protection now. Hot waves of shame wash through me. I cannot hear what Teacher is saying to me, her lips move silently like a fish mouth under water. I cannot hear . . .

. . . I cannot hear her, only the voice of my father. At the dinner table, talking about them: "Niggers. That's what they are. Niggers. Stupid animals."

He smells of martinis, and he is angry. "Junglebunnies, breed like animals to get their welfare checks. My money. MY money. Stupid, lazy, no-good Niggers."

I had thought, I had thought . . .

CHAPTER 6

JEANIE

It broke her heart when they took away her little gray dog. They said they had to. They said the dog was peeing all over the house. But then they took away the house, too. So, she wondered, why didn't they just take the house and leave the dog with her? She didn't need any house, if it couldn't be the one she'd been in for the last sixty years. That was the only house she cared about.

They also took her sherry. All she ever had was a little glass or two at lunch. But they took it away and told her she couldn't have anything like that in the nursing home.

Well, she reasoned, at least they hadn't taken her husband. Small consolation, seeing as for the past three years he had been so confused that he believed himself more often than not to be on the Wisconsin farm of his childhood.

He approached her now. "Well, Nellie, I'm going out to collect the eggs," he said with a wink. "Want to come along?"

"No, Gerben," she said crossly. "You're not on a farm anymore. This is Minneapolis. You're in a nursing home with me. Your wife. Jeanie."

"Well, all right, Nellie. I'll be back before sunup, my love."

Gerben left. She knew that he couldn't get out of the building, that a staff member would find him wandering and bring him back to their little room. Their little room that she hated.

Jeanie wept . . . and wondered what to do. It was unbearably lonely, especially without the little gray dog. She felt so sad inside. The hours seemed to take forever to go by. She could not imagine how to live like this.

Around dusk, Gerben came to her again. "Mama, I'm going to milk the cows. Want to come along?"

Jeanie was about to be cross again but changed her mind. She surprised herself. She replied, "Yes, dear, let me get my sweater on."

She put her sweater on. She took Gerben by the hand. She didn't bother with the key, and actually, it thrilled her to hear the room door click shut and lock.

Together they went down the hall. Together they went over the hill, to the place where the cows come home.

CHAPTER 7
PHARAOH'S DAUGHTER

Cricket Wren. Her real name is Katherine, but she is tiny, and her mother and father call her Cricket. Her mother is Margaret Wren, the local librarian. Her father, Fred Wren, doesn't have a necktie-job, but he has read a great many books from where he sits in the worn wood chair at the kitchen table. His experiments with homemade beer stand in smooth brown bottles along the edge of the kitchen floor near his feet.

The Wrens all live together in a tiny, pleasant house. Cricket's room is a closet with a tiny bunk bed in it. Just her size.

Cricket Wren is my brand new first-grade friend. She shows me the best parts of her house. A cricket cage from China, a wood carving of a woman with long skinny breasts, from Africa. Books stacked everywhere.

We go ice-skating. Cricket Wren can skate, but she doesn't know how to stop. I can barely skate. She shows me that, and then she shows me her new idea about how to stop by flying fearlessly into the drifts at the edge of the rink. We skate and fly, skate and fly all afternoon. It seems like the most fun I have ever had.

We have dinner at Cricket Wren's house. Ravioli from cans, fixed by her father. Then we play checkers, and then we go to bed, she and I, in the tiny bunk bed.

Just before sleep comes to me, I dangle my arm down from the top bunk and touch Cricket Wren ever so lightly on the shoulder. Just to make sure she is really there.

CHAPTER 8
FAY

Fay was one of the most beautiful women. Not fake-beautiful, like the women on beer or car ads, but real-beautiful, as in strong beautiful, big beautiful, smart and tender and tough together beautiful. She came from a big, complicated Catholic family, about thirty-five altogether, who swooped in every holiday to eat together on a cloth-covered piece of plywood that ran between the living room and the dining room of her big house. The big house that she wouldn't give up without a fight, even though the neighborhood had started to crumble around it.

By day, Fay taught single, teen-age mothers how to eat right and feed their babies right. She wooed them off their standard fare of chips, smokes, and cokes, and had a good time with them, making things from cans of refried beans and cheese and rice and tuna. Things with names that made you feel like you'd accomplished something once you'd made them. Names like Sunday Supper Enchilada Bake. Or, All-in-One Tuna Treat. Food a young mother could take some pride in.

And that was just by day. By night, Fay guarded her brood of kids, rumpled her tired husband's hair, and chaired the neighborhood Crime Committee. She called public meetings with city officials, demanded that absentee landlords explain their lead paint preferences in front of everybody and answer why the 911 calls just kept rolling in.

Fay had connections. Lots of connections. The neighborhood pimp, who also dealt drugs, moved his business elsewhere when someone secretly gashed the smooth, metallic pink thigh of his vintage Cadillac. Fay acted dumb about that. Probably she wasn't.

Now that's beautiful, isn't it.

CHAPTER 9

PHARAOH'S DAUGHTER

I am not allowed to ride my bike off the block. I am only allowed to ride it around the block. So I do, sometimes for hours, twenty or thirty times in a row. Alone.

I watch, as I circle the block, for other children who might come out to play with me, in the meantime making up little games to the rhythm of the pedal pumps: Can I name a state, or a flower or a fruit, for every letter of the alphabet? Can I remember all twelve reindeer or all seven dwarves?

It is spring. Something good happens besides the the tiny new bits of leaves and tulips popping out. Something good, besides the sweet smell of thawing dirt. Our teacher, who is huge enough to stare at for a long time, instructs us all to bring our bikes to school. This is for the fourth-grade Bicycle Safety Test on Thursday. She gives each of us a permission slip to be signed by our parents.

A chance to ride my bike off the block! Jim, the traffic cop, who crosses all the children over Main Street after school, can see that I'm excited, waving my permission slip in the warm spring air. "What is it, what is it?" he asks.

I tell him it's a surprise, a secret for now. "Just watch for me on Thursday. You'll see!"

Thursday morning is warm and bright blue. The buds seem ready to burst, the birds are noisy. I am riding my bike to school, riding it right off the block, riding it straight in a line down Garfield Avenue, left on Oak, right on First Street, and across Main.

"Now stay on the sidewalk," I sing to myself, "and look for the driveways, watch for the bumps, hold on with both hands, don't hit first-graders, stop at the corners. Yes, I am riding my bike, right off the block, riding it all the way to school!"

I pedal past Jim like a happy bicycle ballerina, and he waves and winks. I park my bike in the metal rack, crowding it in with all the others. Just like the others at last.

The Bicycle Safety Test site has sprung up overnight on the blacktop playground. It is like a little city. Roads are marked with yellow lines, some one-way, some dead-end, some crossing danger-ously over white-paint railroad tracks, creating every chance for young bikers to practice their skills. There are street signs and stop signs, yields, cardboard box skyscrapers, pretend traffic-signal lights — a full world.

When my turn comes, I take it very seriously, watching for the traffic lights, signaling the turns each and every one. I am filled, overjoyed, almost overwhelmed, with the forbidden fruit of my own independence.

The Safety Test is far too short for my liking. Before I know it, the final stretch is all that lies ahead. I pick up speed toward the finish line, pedaling hard, pedaling harder, flying straight into the blur of the moment, until, until . . . no, oh no, where has she come from? How could I have missed her?

Just inches from my whirling wheels looms my huge fourth-grade teacher, her face filled with terror. I slam on the brakes, but not soon enough, and crash sideways into her, knocking her down in a screaming heap onto the blacktop.

It is over. All over. I have sought to navigate the larger world, and crashed.

CHAPTER 10

SISSY

Sissy was a white girl who fell in love with a Mexican man, and they got married and had a passel of sweet, beautiful, pale brown babies before either of them knew exactly what had happened. It was a good kind of love.

Then times got hard, so they tried moving South and they tried moving North and they tried moving in with her mother. What a disaster that was. And then he left them for a while, and then he came back. There just wasn't enough of this or that, mostly not enough money.

Sissy worked first shift, then he'd work second or third, and that way someone was always home watching the babies, even though Sissy and her husband never saw each other much except when one or the other was too tired to even smile.

Sissy hid her spirit from the world so that only he and the kids were even exposed to it, but it's doubtful they took notice anyway.

Until her employer made a little mistake.

Sissy was in telephone sales. It had looked like a good job, mostly because it included health insurance for her kids. Until she discovered that her boss was running a scam on her, pocketing her paycheck's insurance deductions and not backing up her policy.

On paper, it said she had eighty-percent coverage if this happened, and one-hundred-percent coverage if that happened. But in reality, she didn't have any coverage at all. None.

If she had carried one of her babies with a busted leg or a skull cracked open or a case of pneumonia into a clinic, they'd have thumbed through the files and said, "Sorry, lady, you and yours just don't exist."

Well, one thing led to another. Because her family couldn't afford to miss her paychecks, not even one, she first tried to get it straight with her boss in a polite kind of way. When that didn't work, she tried to get the other employees in on it, but they didn't have kids and they didn't care, and there were only two others, anyway. So then she tried legal means, but in cases like hers, it takes money to make money unless you're experienced. Which she wasn't. Or maybe her husband was undocumented. She didn't say. She just said nothing worked.

So, in the end, she quit. On a Monday night it was. She had tried lots of ways to get some people on her side, and nobody seemed to be there, so she chose dignity over money and walked.

On Tuesday morning, though, she was back. In a picket line. A picket line of her own creation. In the picket line was herself and her passel of babies getting bigger all the time. The big ones watched the little ones while she stood there all day with her own sign upon which she had carefully lettered her own truth. And every child of hers could see that their mother would not be pushed around.

Which is worth a lot.

CHAPTER 11
PHARAOH'S DAUGHTER

They have given me the long, silver flute for my tenth birthday, not knowing what will happen, likely not concerned.

I blow into the silver flute and find that threads of sound spin out into the silence, threads of beautiful colors. I blow and blow . . . a weaver.

I blow and I blow into the long, silver flute. Whole tapestries of bright joy, deep blue sorrow, and golden calm unravel from my contracting lungs. All unspoken stories become told in images of sound, images that fill the silence only for a moment and then are gone.

I can tell it. I can tell it all, breathweaving from the silver flute, and no one ever knows. I mourn, I scream, I laugh long and full of purple. Bring beauty from wounds, patterns from chaos. Spin one million angel wings into the swell of a crescendo.

Sometimes they ask what I am doing up there in my room, the door closed, hour upon hour. More often, they don't notice.

CHAPTER 12
LASHELLA

LaShella sometimes fell asleep when she didn't mean to. She would get home from work, set her bag in the hall, lower her tired bones down onto the sofa, and fall asleep. Instantly. Sitting straight up.

LaShella did not fall asleep like that because of some complicated medical problem that took a team of specialists to diagnose. She fell asleep because she was tired. Bone-deep tired.

Bone-deep tired because she just wouldn't quit.

For one thing, there was work. Had to work. Work meant winter coats for the kids, bologna or better in the fridge, sometimes flowers in a vase on the kitchen table. Independence. Other things too complex and numerous to mention. Had to work.

Then there was church. Had to go to church. Praise God, praise Jesus, love thy neighbor, teach Sunday School, make baked beans for the potluck. Had to do that.

And there was the city. Had to do her part, heart and mind and soul. She specialized in taking on the school system, and nobody dared ignore her, all the way up to the superintendent. Had to do that, so all the children would get what they needed.

Then there were her own children. Had to be cared for. Had to be. Touched, talked to, hugged again and again, no matter how old they got. Had to be watched over tenderly. "How's your homework coming? Why aren't you home on time?

How did Geometry go today?"

Had to be.

Bone-deep tired. Wouldn't quit.

When her youngest child, Kathy, showed an interest in color and art, LaShella bought some chalk and some excellent paper. Kathy drew and drew. She drew a large picture in deep, calm greens and blues. A picture of a mother duck, deftly leading her ducklings into the water. The one at the end was holding back a little, but anybody could tell it was going to make it. Going to launch itself into the cool, blue pool and swim someday, with full skill and grace.

Kathy gave it to LaShella on Mother's Day. Together, soon afterward, they packed it carefully and took it with them on a bus to the nicest department store in town.

They rode the escalator to the floor where consultation on interior decor was done. "We need this framed," said LaShella with authority, spreading out the ducks and the pond on a large, flat table.

The picture hangs in the living room now. LaShella still hasn't quit. Still exhausts herself. Still falls asleep when she sits on the sofa, falls asleep in front of the beautiful picture of the ducks in the pond. Dreaming in deeper greens and blues now. In deeper calm. Deeper hope and faith. Dreaming of the last duckling tipping itself bravely into the water, spreading its little webbed feet, and finding its way.

CHAPTER 13
PHARAOH'S DAUGHTER

In the dream I have a baby sister, years younger than myself. She clings to me, wrapped round me with her legs locked at the base of my spine. I hold her there with ease, as though I have done so for a long, long time.

She is beautiful, the sister in the dream. Her white, white hair swirls in soft tangled masses round her face like a halo. Her skin is a translucent pink.

In the dream I seem not beautiful like her, but ugly — pole gray, pole skinny. My hair is bound in a greasy knot, and shadows flutter like slow moths around me, along my cheekbones and at the nape of my neck.

The door hinges are noisy. They are cruel. They wheeze, cackle like witches in the darkness. Is it a dream? Is it a dream? Where is my baby sister? Where is she? I hear the hinges and panic. I scream silently, Where is she? For we have somehow become separated, and I must not, must not, lose her. Where is she? Where is she?

Who is coming? Who is coming into the room? The door hinges tell me that he is coming. The door hinges are cruel. They laugh and let him in.

But there is no place to go. No place to go. I cannot breathe, cannot move. There is only the bed, and he is coming, coming to the bed, no place to go, help me, please help me.

Where is my baby sister? I have lost her. Is it a dream?

Here she is, beside me, within me. I watch. He hurts her, he hurts her, he hurts her, but I cannot stop him, I am too weak and gray.

He is gone, and then I am gone, far away. I do not feel anything. I do not know anything. Is it a dream?

He is gone, and she is bleeding. I must be quick. I gather her to me and carry her down the stairs, dark and narrow, into the basement. She is slung limp over my back, and her arms flop against me like dead arms.

Is it a dream? My baby sister is bleeding. I lay her down on the smooth concrete, take her by the ankles, and drag her toward the train table, a thin, bright ribbon of blood behind her.

The train table is large and low. Nobody has used it for years. He had built it himself, long ago. Had built it lovingly, perhaps, painted it a bright grassy green and glued on some bushes and trees. Made it real.

Town stations stand here and there, and little people. Tiny smiling mothers with children, waiting on platforms for their husbands to arrive on the evening train from work.

And houses. Houses all in neat rows, and each with painted yellow windows lit from the inside all the time. And stores. A candy store, a grocery store with tiny watermelons in the window.

I have loved the train table. Hours I've spent, gazing at its intricacy and orderliness, wondering whether to spend my allowance at the candy store or the grocer. Wondering which of the tiny smiling mothers is mine.

But in the dream, the surface of the train table barely exists. It is beneath the surface, beneath it, that we must go. Beneath it, into the deep hollow of space where only children can fit.

I pull my baby sister out of sight of everything and hold her. His boot heels boom above us, maybe in the kitchen now, quick and staggering, then slow. But we are safe.

I am safe. Safe in a deep and silent place. Safe from the cruel, laughing, cackling hinges, safe from being hurt any more.

And then, in time, the dream is over. There is no safe space for me, not all the world over. There is no halo-haired small sister to protect. Only myself. Only myself.

CHAPTER 14

CAT

First, the others.

Lola was the motel cook, an overweight high school kid who wanted to get away from her big family. She had lots of pimples.

Roxy, Lola's friend, worked at the motel, too. He brought her on as a waitress. She made a good one because she was skinny and fit between the tables well. Never mind the buck teeth.

There was also a college kid whose mother he'd known once. Feeling obliged, he took Dana on as a chamber maid, even though she was bookish and distracted, which made her bad for this kind of thing.

Now. Cat. She was full-blooded Sioux, short and muscular, with black eyes and black hair. She was fast. Very fast. You put her in a bathroom, it sparkled in just minutes. She could do eighteen in an hour. The people following her, changing sheets and vacuuming, couldn't keep up. She's be smoking a Kool at the end of the row as they made their way around the bend.

Treasure, the one with the heavy sexy lips, the heavy make-up, and the sexy blouses, was his wife. She stayed with him in the main lodge, with nothing to do, since he didn't want her working. Mostly she lounged around in their bedroom amidst the mirrors and feathers, doing her nails and snapping gum.

All the other girls stayed in a cabin with a wood stove and a record player. They ate in the restaurant and worked ten, maybe twelve, hours a day. Seven days a week.

Except Cat. Cat stayed in a separate cabin with her man, Jim, and her two baby girls. Not allowed in the restaurant, she cooked on the wood stove. Jim worked as a hired hand days and went hunting at night in his pick-up truck, up and down the mountain.

Before sunup, the smell of slow cooked wild-animal stew would be rising from their chimney.

Cat's one baby girl toddled after Cat while she worked. The other, younger, stayed in an old crib in the cabin by herself. Sometimes she wailed and wailed, but there was nothing anyone could do.

So. That was who he had around. One night in the bar, he let slip that he intended to get into everyone's panties by Labor Day, which he almost did. He was hard for the girls to get away from.

Cat was the one he couldn't get his hands on, though, which of course he covered up by saying he wouldn't go near a dirty, stinking Indian anyway.

The trouble started when a motel guest reported that her brooch had been taken from her bathroom. Reputation at stake, he called them all together, except Cat. He knew Cat had the thing somewhere in her cabin, he told them, adding in some of his other opinions about rotten drunk Indians, dirty lying cheating Indians, never trust an Indian, and so on and so forth.

He told them what to do. Roxy was to win Cat's confidence and Dana was to search Cat's cabin while she was out cleaning. Treasure was to call in the authorities on child neglect.

One way or another, they'd get her. And he would be watching.

It never occurred to him that they might protect her. Never came to mind that they cared for one another, wouldn't betray one another. Certainly not over something like a brooch.

But by the time the sheriff roared up the mountain, prepped for an arrest, she was gone. No trace. No trace of Cat or Jim, or the two baby girls or the stew pot or the pick-up. No trace of the brooch either. Nothing but a smoky cabin and the laughing ghost of a full-blooded Sioux Indian woman faster than you could imagine.

He was purple with rage. "How could you girls be so stupid!"

Treasure just stood there, smiling vaguely. Lola and Roxy stared at the ground in silence. Dana covered her face with her hands.

"Stupid, stupid, STUPID girls."

The girls had to work harder with Cat gone. All except Treasure, that is. But they did all right. They did all right.

CHAPTER 15

PHARAOH'S DAUGHTER

I sit through the dinner, eat what she gives me. She always gives me more than she gives herself because she doesn't want me to be thinner than she, though she'd never say that. It makes her jealous that I am. And she knows he'll make me eat it all. He always has. I don't even challenge that anymore.

She thinks she's in control then. But she isn't in control. And he isn't in control, either. I am in control.

I eat what she gives me. It goes down like poison. All these years she has used this food as the symbol of her love, the token of her motherly presence. But she doesn't fool me. Poison. It's nothing but poison.

After dinner I quietly clear the dishes while they start in on their after-dinner drinks. As a little girl, I hated the after-dinner drinks, the long hours of after-dinner drinks. They made me sad.

But now the after-dinner drinks are my friends. They give me a window through which to slip away unobserved. Likewise, the dirty dishes. And naturally everyone always says, "What a lovely young woman, picking up after dinner without even being asked."

Good. Good. If they believe that, I'm all the more in control.

In my room I cannot sit, cannot study or read a book, cannot even play the long, silver flute anymore, until I have rid myself of the poison. They can put what they want on my plate. Drink their after-dinner drinks for eternity, stumble around, act nasty or weepy or sloppy all they want, but they can't control me. I control me. My body is my territory, my land, my temple. My only temple. And I, powerful queen of the temple of my body, will have no poison within it.

And so the cleansing ritual begins. Thousands of times I touch my toes. Then jumping jacks, sit-ups, push-ups, chin-ups, twists, running in place, running in place, running in place. A complex purification rite that purges my interior of all the poison, of all the food that is called a gesture of love and that I know, I know, is nothing more than a selfish, sinful, hateful lie.

It takes three hours. Three hours every night. The queen is willful, determined to stay in control. She wants the body lean as bone, no soft curves. Wants it hard, pure. Wants it to fly in the face of their poison. And the more they insist, the more they heap food on the plate and command that it be eaten, the more determined she becomes to diminish the body down to nothing but purity. She will purge it. She will rid it of the evil of all so-called sustenance. This is more important to the furious, powerful queen than life itself. Believe it: She would rather die than fail.

Running in place, running in place, running in place.

CHAPTER 16

MARGARET LOUISE

Margaret Louise said she loved dinner parties. And she actually thought she did. She even invited lots of people to dinner parties. But she hated dinner parties. She just didn't know it at first.

It would happen like this. First, she would start thumbing through her collection of French cookbooks, books with sensual photographs of prime rib and petits fours and steamed, marinated artichokes. With her slender, diamonded fingers wrapped around the delicate stem of a wine glass, she would envision a lovely menu and invite some lovely people for a certain night. Often people from her husband's firm or certain neighbors.

And then, the day of. She would set the table herself, perhaps with a pink linen cloth and an ivory lace runner, the Wedgwood, the silver, soon to sparkle like money in the candlelight. A single rose in hand-blown glass or, sometimes, something more unusual. Something Oriental, say, or just unexpected.

And then the shopping, all in separate little shops. The bread, fresh and crusty, from one. Fine cheeses from another, wine from a third, meat or fresh fish from a fourth.

And it would indeed be a lovely time for everybody. But when the guests had all been waved off and the candles snuffed, Margaret Louise would steal away to the third-floor bathroom where nobody knew what she did. Thrusting her lovely diamonded fingers down her throat, she would vomit it all out in a monumental purge — the meat, the wine, the fish, the lovely, lovely artichokes, the pressure, the boredom, the impossible need for perfection that cursed her every moment of every hour, the hatred she felt for her stupid, egocentric husband and his stupid, egocentric business partners and their dull wives, the deep and relentless hatred of her own body, the deep and relentless hatred of her own meaningless thoughts, the rigidity of her daily existence, the prison of her despair, the self-hatred, the self-hatred, the self-hatred.

There came a time when no purge was sufficient to rid her of the pain inside. Gradually, the pain began to take over. It made her afraid to go outside. It crowded her into her third-floor bedroom, where she huddled for hours. Her husband didn't really notice that anything was so wrong until the day he found her curled up in a corner there, a fetus in a womb of suffering, unable to move. She could not speak. He called the doctor. Had her taken to the seventh floor of St. Mary's Hospital.

In the days of treatment and care that followed, Margaret Louise's old world shattered. Wedgwood hitting concrete. And the radical, frightening, redeeming freedom that followed allowed her to form some new, far gentler habits. A fondness for bus rides. For small talk with those who sat next to her. A fondness for cheeseburgers. For lilacs wild by the side of the road.

CHAPTER 17

PHARAOH'S DAUGHTER

I *sit in the black plastic chair before the vast mahogany desk of the psychologist at the college health service. On his desk, he has a picture of himself next to his wife, who is in a riding outfit, sitting on a dapple horse.*

He seems kind enough, the psychologist. His hair is wild, his necktie crooked and friendly. But I have held myself private within the temple for such a long time, I've become unsure of how to speak. I'm only here because death has seemed so inviting lately.

"What is it?" He leans back in his chair that tips and twirls.

"It's. It's. It's . . . my body, my body feels so ugly, no matter what. No matter what I do . . ."

"What do you do?"

"Well, I run. Every night. I run. And then I swim. Over at the women's gym, you know. I swim. And sometimes. And sometimes. When I don't run or swim. Sometimes I just make myself throw up."

"If I may ask, do you by any chance throw up in the women's bathroom on the first floor of Myer's Hall? They've reported to me that vomit is consistently being found there by the custodian."

"Well. No. I don't vomit there. My dorm room. Has a bathroom attached. Anyway. I'm neat, also. I have a roommate."

"Feeling a lot of pressure here at school?"

"Yes."

"First time away from home?"

"Yes."

"Listen, a lot of students I see talk about the pressure, believe

me. A new level of independence, all the freedom. And let's face it, the expectation to perform at schools like this is pretty intense. I mean, back in high school, most of you were at the top of the academic heap, and now here you are competing with each other. Pretty stressful. Right?"

"Yes. Stressful."

"All that exercise should be doing the job, though, for the stress. I often recommend exercise. But for you, the need might be to really just slow down. Is that it? Are you having trouble slowing down?"

"Well. I. I. Yes. I can't slow down."

"I think I have something here that may help. Have you got a little cassette player here at school?"

"Yes."

"Well, let me give you this relaxation tape. I recommend that you listen to it at least once a day."

"Once a day . . ."

"Yes. Maybe in the morning, when you wake up. Or when things get bad. You know your body is really very proportionate. You needn't worry about being overweight. You're fine, just as you are. Maybe even underweight. Believe me. You just need to learn how to relax a little bit. Believe me, it's a common thing during the freshman year."

"Yes. Well."

"There's the smile! Good! But I want you to know that you are welcome to come back here any time if things don't get better. That's what I'm here for, and I'd be glad to see you again. These transitions are not always easy."

"No. I mean, yes. That's right. I mean, thank you. I'll try."

I begin moving toward the door.

I leave the health service building and find myself breaking into a run. I am running now, running and running. I am running myself to Death. Her arms encircling me, would they not be tender? Would they not be gentler, infinitely more so, than the driven temple queen's? Than my mother's? My father's? Do they not already hold and rock the old black dog? Do they not await, even now, the halo-haired child of the dream?

I am running myself to Death, and the one thing I have, to stop myself from getting there, thanks to the psychologist at the college health service, is a relaxation tape.

CHAPTER 18

LAURA

Vice-Chair of the Board, she stood at the front of the room near the two displays about which she was leading the discussion. As people spoke, she summarized, interpreted, pushed where she needed to push, encouraged where she saw fit. The Chair himself at one point questioned her discretion. She brushed him aside like a crumb on a carpet, politely, of course. Her large, lovely eyes ended the exchange with a slow blink.

The arch of Laura's brow, the strong, slender curve of her neck, the grace of her poised arm, the distinct quietude of her voice, all bespoke a queen's eloquence. There was very little — perhaps nothing — to suggest the extent to which she had been shoved around, beaten up, abused, or held down.

Yet she had been. Behind the innocuous-seeming white front door of the lovely suburban house of her childhood, someone had hurt her. She was smart, so it didn't take much for her to learn. A slap here, a welt there, and then all it took was words.

Words there had been aplenty — screamed words, abusing words.

"I could just kill you, you stupid child!"

"You better watch out, or I'm gonna shake you, shake you till your teeth rattle!"

"Do it, or I'll snatch you baldheaded, you stupid little girl."

"Can't you do anything right? Why are you so stupid?"

These words, from her own mother's twisted, angry

mouth, had worked their way on her, diminished her inside, made her wish she could just disappear, made her believe that she was nothing — worthy of nothing, deserving of nothing, capable of nothing. For years and years she had lived in fear, perpetually flinched for the blow that would surely come, for the words that would name her worthlessness.

On rare occasions a tuft of grass will push its way through concrete, as unlikely as it sounds. When the concrete is first poured, it seems so hard and strong, much stronger than any tiny seeds it might cover up. But time can bring change. The concrete, in all its brittle strength, will crack and buckle. The seeds, ever hungry for sun and life, will begin to grow. They will push their way through, laboring arduously on a slow miracle.

That's what Laura is. A slow miracle.

CHAPTER 19

PHARAOH'S DAUGHTER

No.

There are better ways.
Better than running.
Drinking.
The first shot is the only evil-seeming one, and the minute it hits, sliding down the gullet like ice on fire, the minute it hits, it numbs the guilt like a kind of Novocaine.

The next round of shots numbs the self-hatred, and this still in solitude. Blessed release, the driven queen finally tumbles in schizophrenic confusion, damn her.

The next round of shots facilitates conversation, as they say. Isn't that funny, to finally find words, after all these years: yes, hello, is that right, oh me, oh my, you don't say, how very very fascinating, yes yes yes. Words like stale water over a ruptured dam, like rhythms unleashed from some long lost internal drum. Words pouring out in syncopation, splish splash doo dah walla walla bing bang.

The next round of shots numbs memory. Getting there, getting there.

But the final round. The final round. Yes. Numbs all consciousness. The final round, as good as death, as deep as death, as blind and deaf and dumb as death, but without all the blood and guts. The final round, yes. Death for the uncourageous, the chicken-hearted, those too afraid to really do it. Yes. The final round, spent at the bottom of a stairwell somewhere, legs akimbo, or in the wrong bed, or stretched across a snowbank like a stinking fish on ice. The final round, yes it is, yes it is as good as death and maybe cheaper. What do you want for three ninety-eight a bottle, honey?

CHAPTER 20

TAMI

Growing up, Tami had nothing to remind her that she was a child of God. No father who doted, no mother who fussed even a tiny bit or treated her with tenderness at all, for that matter. Her two brothers, they didn't care about her. Her older sister didn't either. Tami had nothing. Nothing.

So that when she saw him, Maurice that is, on the city bus, and decided he was the one for her, she had nothing to lose.

Riding the city bus on the way to school, sitting within his sight, she had watched him for months, smiling when he looked, flirting here and there. Determined. She had gotten him, too. Maurice. She had gotten him and had his babies, and he was all hers, and she knew heaven when his arms held her tight.

Now when he got tangled up with another woman, a girl who worked at a downtown bank, Tami knew what had to be: The lady had to die.

It was easy. Tami was good at watching Maurice, and she saw him take his other woman to lunch. Tami waited in the lobby of the fifth floor of the bank building, waited for Maurice to bring the lady back. She'd kill them both. Eight-months pregnant, she clutched the crocheted baby blanket she was making and felt the fires of unleashed rage push through her veins.

It was almost as if Maurice had a sixth sense: He was nowhere in sight when the other woman stepped off the elevator from lunch, spike-heels and all. Tami lunged at her from behind, grabbed a wad of high-style bouffant, threw her by the hair up into the air, and then whacked her down again and started swinging.

The security guards were on her in a flash, grabbing her muscular, angry arms as best they could, disentangling her from her foe, hushing her, threatening to call the cops. After messing them up some, Tami knew she'd made her point. Nostrils flaring with fury, she picked up her crocheting off the carpet and stalked onto the open elevator.

You'd think Maurice would have learned something from that. Oh, he was faithful for a while. Until the baby was born. But then it happened again. Another lady came along and distracted him from Tami.

This time, Tami meant business. She found the woman in a bar. Took her outside in the alley, ready to fight to the death. Let her have it, a fist right in her nasty, dirty face. But Maurice's new lady had a single-edge razor on her, and she started cutting up Tami from head to toe. Cut her ear half off. A gentleman who had been only driving by, driving slowly down the alley in his Chevy, saw the blood and the dangling ear, threw Tami in his back seat, and headed straight to the hospital.

Blood was squirting out of Tami and soaking into his upholstery. Blood was smeared all over everything. Blood filled her eyes, she couldn't see. But even then she didn't know she was cut. She hit the emergency room dazed, still confused about what had happened to her. Still confused about Maurice and love and violence and other women and babies and just getting by in this cold, dirty life.

Some thought she wouldn't make it. Some thought she wasn't going to figure it all out.

They were wrong.

CHAPTER 21

PHARAOH'S DAUGHTER

There is a tiny, tiny explosion of life in me. I can feel it. My period is late.

I am not sure how it has happened. Might have been the man I wanted cocaine from. Or the nicer, gentler one, down from up north on a Saturday night. Might have been the one who laughed and laughed when the condom split. Might have been one I can't remember, one of the endless, faceless final-rounders.

What does it matter? Something tiny, something sacred, the living spark of the halo-haired child, is buried deep inside me. And there is only one thing to do and that is to kill it.

The abortion clinic waiting room could be anywhere. Could be the waiting room of the college health service. The dentist's. Except it's all women. Women alone together. We do not speak to one another but sit in silence, all of us, each bearers of terrifying tidings.

When my turn comes, the nurse takes me to a little room. We will have a little meeting with the doctor first, a little talk, and some kind of release form.

The doctor seems kind enough. He does. He is concerned about the open wounds on my face. There are at least two or three of them, they have been there for weeks. I do not know what to call them, I have not been able to make them heal. He gently explains that he is worried about performing an abortion without knowing what they are, medically.

Medically. The words sear me somehow, burn my last hopes to cinder. Numbly I sit. Worried.

Then, oddly, tears come. The first tears in years. They come slowly at first, then more. Unexpected. Unwelcome. Tears for this woundedness and all old wounds, tears stinging my gaping, leprous cheeks and staining the release form before me. Tears for the little girl having her stomach pumped, the dead old black dog, the young woman who could not run hard enough.

Everything condensed now into a single pinpoint of time.

This is it, this is it, the moment I must speak, the truth I must finally utter, this is it, there is no more, not another moment, not another hope, not another chance.

"Doctor. The sores are the rottenness, Doctor. They are just the rottenness. Inside of me, coming out. It is coming out of me, coming out where it can, there is so much of it, my skin can't hold it in any more.

"Doctor. I cannot keep a human life in all this rottenness. It would be all poisoned, mutilated. It would suffer and suffer. I cannot do it, I cannot. If you can't do this abortion, I know what will happen. I know what will happen. I will do it myself, by killing myself, and soon. Soon. Doctor, I cannot help myself anymore."

The doctor then does something unexpected. He puts down his pen and takes my hand. He takes my hand and holds it. Pats it a little bit. Holds it in wordless tenderness for a long, long time, all the long while that I weep.

"So. I will perform the abortion then. But you must promise me something. You must promise me that if I do it, you will not go on like this. No more of this. No more."

Some kind of holiness, some kind of untold healing, passes from his hand into mine. I feel it move from him to deep inside me where my wounded soul lies curled in fetal folds. I feel it, like a love-cast rescue rope, as surely as I am alive. It gives me the strength to say the promise.

"Yes. I promise. I will not go on like this."

And so it is, that the hands of this doctor whose name I do not know, whose hands have such power to heal me, surgically remove the very life from me that I may live.

And so it is, that I leave the abortion clinic. Not with great hope or faith or strength, but with a fragile wish to evade death. And a promise to keep.

CHAPTER 22

MARSHA AND RUTHY

First, Marsha had Ruthy, then Jay, then Beau, and that was enough for a woman on her own. It took her awhile, but she got it all together. Got a house, got a job, a church, friends. Got a rhythm going where she didn't have to take Nothing from Nobody.

And then, boom, she was pregnant again.

She moaned and groaned some, but only for a little while. It just wasn't her style.

Her belly began to swell. Ruthy was ten years old, and curious. She brought her mother meat sandwiches, cooked noodles for the others, and asked, "Mama, can I be there when the baby's born?"

Marsha thought, Why not?

On the night she went into labor, Ruthy was at a slumber party. Marsha got the neighbor girl in to take care of the others, swung by and picked up Ruthy in a taxi, and headed for the hospital.

The birth was a hard one. Marsha, who usually pushed her babies out with a grunt or two, was in labor for hours. Ruthy, short on sleep, began to fuss. "This is boring, I'm hungry, where's the baby?"

Marsha didn't like being in labor so long, it hurt like crazy, and she couldn't stand the whining. "What do you want, child, fireworks? Shush now. When a woman's having a baby, nothing else matters except having the baby. Someday your turn will come. So you be quiet now. And say, could you bring me some ice?"

Ruthy fed her mother ice. Even for her whining, she was a good, good child, good to the core. Before too long she saw that her mother was beginning to grunt and breathe harder. The nurse came in, took a look, and said, "Almost time, Marsha, let me go get the doctor."

Yes, it was almost time, and Ruthy watched with her eyes wide open. They were in there now, the doctor, the nurses. Her mother was making the mysterious, rhythmic noises of birthpain. But always in the lulls, she would say a little some-thing to her Ruthy. Like, "Don't be afraid of me, Ruthy, this is just how it is." Or, "Don't ever let them tell you it doesn't hurt, Ruthy." Or, "Remember this in a few years, Ruthy, when you think sex sounds like all fun." Or just plain, "Hold my hand, Ruthy . . ."

Then, "Get yourself round the end of the bed, Ruthy. The head's coming out!"

Ruthy got herself round the end like her mother told her and watched wide-eyed the recurrence of the old miracle that surpasses all understanding. Watched as they cut the cord, then, cleaned the baby off, and handed it back to her mother. Sat dumbfounded in the chair as Marsha touched the baby, smelled it, put its hair to her cheek, wept, and fell asleep.

When the neighbor girl brought the boys to visit a few hours later, they were wild and excited, smearing their fingers and noses against the glass windows at the hospital nursery, trying to get a glimpse of their new baby sister. "Mama, Mama, we're here! How's the baby? What was it like? What was it like, Ruthy?"

Ruthy's face was something of a mask. She looked solemnly at her mother, choosing with care what she would divulge to these wild manchildren.

"Wasn't much. Kind of boring," said Ruthy nonchalantly, holding her newborn wisdom close to her heart.

She smiled at her mother, who smiled back.

CHAPTER 23
PHARAOH'S DAUGHTER

Well-being comes slowly. I sit in my rocking chair and gaze out the window for hours at a time, sober now, deep in healing thought.

Gradually, gazing, I discern that numbers of old women in hand-stitched embroidery hats cross the street each morning to enter the building across the way.

I ask some questions and find that these are the Hmong refugee grandmothers, coming to class to learn to speak English, departing each morning from the war-torn nets of their extended families to walk together. Many are lone elders, having lost their husbands or brothers or sisters in mountainous Laos or the camps of Thailand.

These are the Hmong refugee grandmothers, the last culture bearers, who stitch out their stories in the Pa Ndau embroidery art of their ancestors, guided by no measure but a sure inner eye. Cars terrify them. Deep in touch with a spirit world from which their very offspring have been severed by American culture, they yearn for the shaman.

These are the Hmong refugee grandmothers, and without knowing why, I want to be with them.

Before my first class, the program director, a younger Hmong woman, tells me just to aim for a good time with them. "Just have a little fun," she explains. "They will die before they need to speak fluent English, but not before they need a little fun. Life has been too hard on them. Too hard."

'Just a little fun' proves difficult, for their lives are so riddled

with loss and death that even the simplest conversational English leads to painful memories.

I try a new tack. Food.

Popcorn, for instance. A good word. A good food. They all like the taste of it, everybody learns to make it. And that leads to other words, too. Like Salt. And Butter. Bowl. Hot. Cheap.

We are on our way together, unlikely fellow travelers, the Hmong refugee grandmothers and myself.

Lesson after lesson, we talk and eat together. Pizza. Cheese pizza. Pepperoni pizza. SUPREME pizza. Big Mac. Fries. CoolWhip. Pumpkin pie. Chocolate chips. Raisins. Ice cream.

Summer comes, and the last day of class. The lesson is Nuts, all kinds of nuts, and a special American-style surprise that I hope will not puzzle or frighten them too much.

Class begins. First, Peanuts. Then Pecans. Walnuts, Hazelnuts, Pistachios, Macadamias. Finally, my surprise.

I hand the can to Lau Her, for she is the leader. "Nuts," I say, trying to look both serious and tender. "A special good-bye for you, a can of nuts." We read the label out loud together: "Nuts."

Lau Her unscrews the lid, and without warning a three-foot-long plastic snake leaps high into the air before her, whizzing just inches past her nose.

It's the old NUT joke! We are laughing. We are laughing and laughing. The tears stream down our faces. We cram the snake back into the can and do it again. Everybody tries it. It is perfect. A real summation, somehow.

We hug one another good-bye. Then the Hmong refugee grandmothers head out the door and across the street together, speaking rapidly now in Hmong, discussing, I imagine, whom to try the Nut joke out on first.

I lock the building, cross the street myself, and return to my rocking chair by the window. I have learned, for the grandmothers have taught me. Isolation is not necessary. And in response to those who disagree, I have even learned what I will say. I will say, "Nuts!"

CHAPTER 24
MACY

By the time her husband, Bud, had reached his deathbed, he had become incontinent, uncomfortable, confused, and entirely ready to be done with it. His last words had been, "This old-age business is not for sissies. I've had enough of it. Don't forget to spread my ashes over the lake. Good-bye."

Forgot, again, to tell her he loved her.

Even so, Macy hadn't wanted him to die. And it was just a mistake that she had left his ashes in an urn on the kitchen counter back in Milwaukee when summer came and it was time to drive to the lake.

Gazing out at the sunset on the lake that first night, though, she remembered and was stricken with a sickening combination of guilt and nausea. After some hesitation, she called a friend back home, and the ashes arrived just a few days later. In an UPS truck.

That night after supper the children and the grand-children gathered round. They each took a custard cup of ashes and set out in the motorboat, Bud's favorite pastime, to the middle of the lake.

His passing, fairly easy for him by the time it arrived, had been nothing but a struggle for Macy and all her kin. They had stumbled numb through the memorial service and the cards with praying hands on them and the casseroles, still pretending that maybe he hadn't gone anywhere in particular.

But these ashes, this gesture of letting the wind take

them over the lake, could not be denied. Tears streaming down their cheeks, young and old alike, they finally said good-bye to Bud as they cast his former self, his lost beloved flesh and bones, across the water. All of them, that is, except Macy, who stubbornly controlled herself.

When they were done, there was silence in the boat for a very long time. And then all of a sudden someone shouted, "Hey, let's go swimming with Bud!"

"Yes, let's go swimming with Grandpa!" the grandchildren echoed. And in this most spirit-filled moment they wildly leapt from the boat for a final swim with Bud. Into the water they flung themselves with all their clothes on, into the brew of his ashes.

All of them, that is, except the widow Macy, who sat grim in the driver's seat, gripping custard cups, her lips held in a tight, pained line.

They all turned at once when the love-cry broke from deep inside her, a sonorous wail it was, from her soul. And then the words:

"You! You! You forgot to say you loved me, you dumb old coot! But I miss you, oh how I miss you, miss you so . . ."

And then, at last, the weeping. The weeping as though she would never stop. The weeping, as her own true love's favorite motorboat rocked and swayed, rocked and swayed to the rhythm of the sunset.

CHAPTER 25

PHARAOH'S DAUGHTER

In late summer, when the black birds are beginning to swoop in southward arcs, I get pregnant and get a job. At the same time.

The pregnancy leaves me speechless with joy. I pluck pears off the tree in the yard, let the juice run silly down my chin. Grab my husband's hand in the middle of the night and put it gently to my belly, whispering, "Can you feel anything yet, James?"

The job is in a junior high school. They are looking for someone to work with the "behavior problems," the potential dropouts. I am to help these kids with their school work and see if I can keep them out of trouble.

September. The leaves on the pear tree begin to turn and drift away. My husband's hand hasn't felt anything yet, nothing shows. My first student strides into class, impeccably dressed, toothpick between his gleaming teeth. One look at him and I know I will love this child.

Benjamin D. has a reputation. He carves swastikas in school desks, and sometimes in his own skin. Swears fearlessly in the face of important people. Refuses homework. Has a file as fat as an unabridged dictionary, full of phrases like "sociopathic tendencies" and "high criminal risk." He is eleven years old.

November. The pear tree stands naked against a clear sky. My husband's hand finally has felt life careening inside me. I walk to school through the bright leaves.

Benjamin D., after a great deal of posing and stancing, has revealed his big secret: He can't read.

Can't read the textbooks, the library books. Can't read the comments teachers have scrawled on his math worksheets. Can't read a thing. And nobody knows it. Nobody even suspects it. He has fooled them all by acting outrageous to distract them.

"Benjamin D.," I say, "believe me, you must be brilliant to have pulled this off. Think about it. You've been in the public schools for seven years, man."

"Oh right. Yeah. That's me. Brilliant. Sure. You bet."

"Do you want to learn how to read?"

Long pause. "Yeah."

"All right. Tomorrow. We'll start."

February. The pear tree is holding tall heaps of white snow high toward an icy sky. Every night I fall asleep with books about babies open against my chest. James gently marks the place and sets them aside.

Benjamin D. and I have tried everything. Sight-word method. Phonics. Flashcards, sandtrays, games. We have gambled our pocket change on five-card stud with three-letter words. Studied street signs. Drilled and practiced and worked, hours each day, yearned and even wept. He's not getting it. Not at all.

He's not getting it, and I can't get him to get it. Benjamin D. is raw with pain; he has taken the risk of his life and failed. Swastikas begin to appear in my classroom, carved on the desks, drawn on the walls. I feel like screaming.

Then I get this idea.

April. The snow is turned to slush, and tiny green buds are pushing from the naked pear tree. James and I head off to birthing class each Thursday evening.

By now, Ben and I have finished at least twenty books. It's been easy. I've simply read each book to him out loud. We began in

February with Black Boy *by Richard Wright. It riveted him to his chair, set his bright mind on fire, whetted his appetite for more.*

From there we went on to other books — Malcolm X, Mohammed Ali, James Baldwin. Ben's mind is deep and complex, and nuance never evades him. He has begun to tell his own stories and proves to be a master at weaving narrative. He has started to produce exceptional line drawings that the Art teacher studies in awe.

Today, though, we are reading a text on aviation, an assignment from the Physics of Aviation class he began last month. He sits absorbed, his head resting in the palms of his hands, eyes closed.

He's getting it. Storing it in memory. Tomorrow, when the teacher says, "Which rule, class, explains the phenomenon of such and such?", his hand will go up, probably ahead of the others.

June. The pear tree is leafy. I am due any time now. It is the last day of school. Benjamin D. will be gone next year, off to a magnet school that specializes in the arts.

"I will miss you. Very much."

"Yeah. Sure. Right." His smile is tender, though, for he knows that I speak to him from my heart.

"The school will be a good place for you. You will do well."

Long pause.

"I have some advice for you. Can I give you some advice?"

"Sure."

"I know you like the Marines, but I hope you think carefully about that. You're an artist. You have all the brilliance, the spiritual depth, of a real artist. I know you're only twelve, but I may not get a chance to give you advice again. So I have to give it now.

"And one more thing. I believe that there will be lots of women who will fall in love with you. Pick one who likes to read. To read out loud. That way you'll be in books for good."

He grins. "Sure," he says. "I'll do that. See you."

I grin back. "See you."

The pear tree blooms. The baby comes. A tiny manchild he, healthy and strong. He has already heard, in utero, a fine array of literature, biography, and fact. I hold him close to my heart.

We name him Benjamin.

CHAPTER 26
RUBY

It is hard to be a prophetess.

The visions first came to Ruby when she was young, sixteen or seventeen years old. They came to her in a place deep behind her heart, a soul world where only gospel had gone before. They came to her in bright blood-red colors, and purples. They came to her in voices, the hot whisper of her God.

She could see futures unfurl. Could see the peony decay before it had even burst open. Could see the man hit his woman's face before he had even conceived of being angry. Could see the bitter shadow of the final holocaust.

Her eyes would become yellow behind the pupils then, and watery. Her voice would become strange, as though her tongue no longer belonged to her, thickened and then moved by something unseen.

Her mother, afraid, had Ruby put away. Because there was no money, she was placed in the state mental institution. There, she prophesied more and more, the visions tumbling from her, spilling into the ears of nurses and strong men in white suits, into the ears of others who rocked and rocked, who cackled and screamed and twirled.

Ruby was a prophetess, and the place behind her heart was aflame, a cauldron foaming and bubbling as though it would never cease.

The world usually ignores a prophetess, and indeed, the

world ignored Ruby. Her mother visited her less and less. The staff learned to turn away.

A younger nurse named Elizabeth, new on staff, sat down next to Ruby. "You in great pain," was what Ruby said to her, without any introduction. "You be suffering, ain't nothing no good for you right now, isn't that so."

The young nurse had miscarried, just days before. She silently gazed at Ruby.

"Don' worry about dat baby. A girl, she name Mary. She wit God, she be all right. Light all around her little body. Now don' you fret about your Mary. She got no pain."

The young nurse felt a tremendous power coming from Ruby, and a tremendous, deep, vibrant compassion. The nurse put her face in her hands.

"An don' worry about you own self," Ruby went on. "Don' worry about it. You got the spirit in you, you be all right. You just need time, child."

The young nurse began to shake with silent sobs.

"Here's what you worry about, child. Worry about that husband o' yours. Now he be weak. He can't take these things. You got to show him the way, child. He never find it on his own."

Ruby took her large outspread hand and laid it gently upon the pained back of the young nurse. Ruby let her hot healing compassion pass down her arm, through her hand, and into the young nurse, filling her with with new power.

When the sobbing subsided, Ruby said, "There now, you can do this. You can do, I know so. The peace of God be in your heart deep, Lizzie child."

The nurse started as though she had been burnt, for the last one to call her Lizzie had been her own mother, ten years dead now. After that, even though she had felt Ruby's great power and had drawn upon it, she stayed away. Anyone could tell the woman was crazy. Just look at the way she foamed at the lips, spewing out her words of fire, acting the idiot.

It is hard to be a prophetess.

CHAPTER 27

PHARAOH'S DAUGHTER

This church is not like any from my childhood. There is no darkness. The huge arched windows that circle the sanctuary are made of clear glass, and the sunlight tumbles in everywhere. The walls are broad and white and plain, the wooden pews worn smooth.

James and I sit in the front pew. Our son rests quietly in the curve of my arm, deep in a dreaminess that only the very young and the very old can comprehend.

This is his Dedication Ceremony. The gathered community encircles us, ready to bless our child, ready to promise that they, too, will value and guide him.

The minister calls us forward.

"What have you named this child?"

"We have named him Benjamin."

The minister pulls a rose from the bouquet at the lectern. Its blossom is heavy and deep red. Its thorns have been stripped off. Stripped off for this very ceremony to symbolize that, within these walls, love is more powerful than suffering. This is the gift of the community to my son, and to all its sons and daughters.

"Benjamin," the minister continues, "we give you this rose, symbol of a beautiful life unfolding."

Benjamin wraps his fat fingers round the thornless stem and joyfully navigates the bloom toward a curious mouth.

I cannot hear the rest. I know that the community is promising to love this child, that James and I are promising to love him, to care for him. That God's own tenderness is being invoked. I know that the minister is gathering Benjamin in strong arms now, holding him high in the bright air, saying his name so stridently and proudly that I am sure even the angels hear.

I know but cannot hear the words clearly or even see clearly, for I am overwhelmed — overwhelmed with joy. And even as Benjamin is blessed, a tiny child, a tiny halo-haired child — deep inside me, or in my memory, or in some cosmic memory of my old woundedness — becomes healed.

CHAPTER 28

MIRIAM AND HER MOTHER-IN-LAW

Miriam was good at doing good things for cheap. So at least once or twice a month she organized her church people to serve a meal at the homeless shelter. Persuaded others not only to give their time and money but also to like giving it.

The only thing that stood a chance of distracting her was when her mother-in-law came to visit. They'd sit at the kitchen table and get so carried away talking that everything else ran a serious risk of getting ignored. Dinners, good deeds, and husbands included.

Which is exactly what happened one cool September day after her mother-in-law had been there about a week. They'd been shopping all afternoon, hitting every deal in town. Now it was dusk, and dinner would just have to be bologna sandwiches. Pretty sweaters and salad twirlers and bargain shampoo lay scattered across the countertop. Miriam and her mother-in-law were enjoying a cup of coffee and a cigarette together when the phone rang.

"Hello, this is the shelter. The folks are in line for dinner. Aren't you supposed to be serving this evening?"

Miriam looked like she'd been hit in the head with a cold fish. "What is it, what is it?" her mother-in-law kept asking as

Miriam shouted things like "Be right over" and "Just hold on" into the phone.

"Ma," she said, hanging up, "Ma! Grab your purse. We gotta go. I'll explain on the way."

While Miriam blasted through the rush-hour traffic, her mother-in-law counted their money. "Twenty-seven dollars and fifty-three cents," she finally announced. "What are we gonna do with it, sweety?"

They pulled into the supermarket and began racing up and down the aisles like a couple in a game-show contest. Hot dogs, buns, cheese, baked beans, onions, chips, pickles, mustard — dinner for fifty.

"Dessert," her mother-in-law insisted. "They gotta have dessert."

"Ma! There isn't money, and there isn't time!" Miriam half-shouted as she ducked into the shortest line.

"Oh yes there is!" her mother-in-law half-shouted back. She grabbed three gallons of ice cream from the cooler, took off her left shoe, and pulled a twenty-dollar bill out from between the sole and the lining. "For emergencies," she added, grinning as though she had just pulled a trick on the whole world.

The folks at the shelter were dog-tired and very hungry. Many of them had not eaten since that time the day before. When Miriam and her mother-in-law came through the door with their arms full of groceries, a cheer rose from the crowd, and many people stepped out of line to help them out.

LaMar sliced onions. Duke set out paper plates, and Filene and her kids began ripping open bags of chips. This was a real break in tradition. Normally, the people being fed stayed out of the kitchen altogether. This was better than that. Miriam didn't need to shout, "Line up, dinner's ready!" because everybody knew it. They'd all played a part. And instead of serving them, she just grabbed a plate herself and sat down with them, hungry as she'd ever been.

It wasn't just a dinner; it was a kind of victory. And Miriam's mother-in-law marked it by cruising from table to table with a scoop in her hand and an ice cream cart at her hip.

"What'll you have?" she asked everywhere she went. "Strawberry? Chocolate? Vanilla? Or would you like one of each, sweety?"

CHAPTER 29

PHARAOH'S DAUGHTER

When the doctor tells me that Benjamin has diabetes, I act tough. This explains the weight loss, the sluggishness, the pallid face, I reason. I set up an appointment with the specialist immediately. The sensible thing.

My toughness, within twenty-four hours, becomes tinged with a pained tenderness, a protectiveness so potent it suffocates. The diabetes requires that he eat just so, and inject insulin just so, and rest and exercise just so. I become the controller — of Just So, Just Right, Right Now, and Never Again. This is my baby, my first-born, even though he is fast approaching six feet tall and thirteen years of age.

James tries to quiet me, but I won't have it. Benjamin has two problems now. His diabetes and his mother. The diabetes brings him hypodermic needles, insulin reactions, vague fears about failed circulation, lost vision. His mother brings him the tyranny of tenderness too much unleashed.

My seminary professors are kind. They wait for the missed assignment, for the bleary-eyed presentation thrown together between doctor appointments and meticulously crafted meal plans. It never comes. I intend to do everything. Be everything. Provide everything. "Don't worry," I insist. "I'm fine."

It is the nun in the bed who finally breaks through to me. She has come to the hospital where I am being trained for chaplaincy. They send me to her, adding that I need to prepare myself for she has just been through surgery for amputation of a finger. Complications of diabetes.

I push my own diabetes issues to the back of my mind and walk into her dimly lit room, prepared to listen to hers.

I find that I am not prepared. Younger than myself, the nun in the bed has already gone blind. Both her legs have already been amputated above the knee, as has her full left arm. On her right arm remains her hand, her thumb, and one lone last finger.

I feel as though I am facing Death itself, the cumulative ravages of diabetes at its cruelest. I mumble a quiet greeting.

"Uh, oh," she says. "A woman! I can tell by the voice. You know, what I really wanted was a priest. A priest for Eucharist. Thought I told 'em that. But that's all right. You'll do, for now. Pull up a chair."

I pull up a chair.

"How are you doing?" I whisper.

"Doing pretty good, pretty good," she sings out. "But you know this cursed diabetes! Just look at me will you? It's like Death coming for me slow, carting me off piece by piece, not to sound flip or anything, but . . . say. Are you crying?"

Yes. I am crying . . .

It spills out, all unprofessional, all inappropriate for a chaplain at a bedside. It spills out, about Benjamin, about me, about tough tenderness, and mother-fear so overwhelming it smothers. Tears, grief, rage. Soul to naked soul we meet, she and I, in the dimness of the light.

"You are feeling what you need to feel," she whispers. "He's dying. I'm dying. We're all dying, and don't let any fast-talking, white-coated doctor tell you otherwise. Yes. Just look at me. We are dying."

I cannot speak.

"The trick is, you've got to stop worrying about him so much,"

she goes on, becoming more matter-of-fact. "If you don't quit that, you'll smother what life he does have. He's a kid! He'd probably rather BE dead some days than not have some kind of junk food that's bad for his diabetes. A life lived in dread of Death is poverty-stricken. A life lived as a dance with Death — even a rough and dangerous dance — is much richer. Let go. Let him dance."

Still, I cannot speak, though my tears have begun to lessen.

"I know, I know. You're worried about him becoming an amputee, losing his limbs like I have. How can a boy dance, if he doesn't have his dancing feet?

"There's something you can do for that, you know. Wash his feet. Just like Jesus did. That's what my mother did, right up until I lost them. Washed them every day. Dried them with a towel. Excellent for the circulation — and the soul. And when you're not washing them, just pretend you are. Pretend it in your mind. You'll feel better."

When Benjamin comes home from school that day, I kiss his cheek. I am washing his feet. When he is extra hungry at dinner, I flex the rigid menu plan and offer more bread. I am washing his feet. When he races out the door with his friends, I don't stop him, for I see that he is dancing. Dancing with Life. Dancing with Death. Dancing with his own two tenderly washed, beloved, joyous diabetic feet.

Dancing.

CHAPTER 30

DEBORAH, POLLY, ELIZA, AND LYDIA

Deborah wiped the baby's bottom, flipped her onto her stomach, and set her in the sun that shone through the living room window. Lydia had come from the orphanage at nine months with a hurtful rash, and it would take time to make it better.

She stood up, then, to tend to Eliza. Eliza was two and liked to put all her clothes on herself − it was a point of pride − but sometimes she got into serious tangles that felt like traps, and then she would turn to her mother for help.

By the time Eliza's arms were through the sleeve holes, Lydia was crying as though her heart would break. The orphanage rash was nothing compared to the orphanage loneliness that she had been forced to experience. There was only one thing to do. Hold her tenderly in the rocking chair and sing to her. Deborah did just that. With a batch of cloth diapers across her lap, just in case.

Eliza played with the toys in the basket for a few minutes and then tried to squash herself into her mother's lap, too. Deborah moved from the rocking chair to the couch, so that there would be room for all three of them. She tried to read a little book about bunnies to Eliza, but Lydia didn't like that, so she tried singing the book to Eliza as though it were a lullaby for Lydia. That worked for a little while − three times through, anyway.

Eliza wanted apple juice. Still holding Lydia, Deborah headed for the kitchen and poured some but didn't get the cup lid snapped on quite firmly enough — it was hard with just one hand — so that when Eliza tipped it, it went all over the kitchen floor.

The phone rang, but nobody answered it.

Lydia pooped.

Was it lunchtime already? Eliza wanted cheese, but there wasn't any. There was yogurt, which Eliza didn't want it but was willing to give it a try, if Mommy would let her hold the spoon all by herself.

Lydia would eat almost anything, that was lucky. Deborah reached up and brushed a Cheerio from her hair.

It didn't take too long to get the girls into their jackets and hats, and Eliza was dancing with excitement about pushing the stroller. By the time they got to the corner, though, Lydia was crying again, and Eliza wanted to ride in the stroller, not push it. Deborah picked up Lydia, kissed her cheek, and pushed Eliza along in the stroller with her other hand.

They got home.

Eliza pooped.

Lydia fell asleep. Then Eliza fell asleep. Then Deborah almost fell asleep but forced herself to get up and work at the computer on her consulting business, though her mind was blurred with exhaustion.

By the time Polly got home from work, Deborah was done in. Polly changed out of her linen suit and put on her jeans, made a clean-up sweep through the living room, and set the table, all the while with Eliza's strong little arms wrapped around her right leg.

"Mama! Mama! Mama! Pick me up!"

Polly picked her up and kissed her cheek.

At dinner, Deborah helped Lydia and Polly helped Eliza. Polly had brought home Chinese take-out.

They ate by candlelight.

CHAPTER 31
PHARAOH'S DAUGHTER

The day before graduation. The day before graduation from seminary. And this has to happen.

I stare at the headline.

"Bruce Smith, Founder of the Minneapolis Poverty Department, Found Dead."

Then the article.

"Although forty-two-year-old Bruce Smith was found dead last night, he lived long enough to realize his dream of establishing a theater company for poor people, the MPD, which presented its first performance recently at First Church on Fremont Avenue.

"Smith, who used the stage name Disney Spielberg, often referred to himself as a trambo, a combination tramp and hobo. The exact cause of Smith's death remains uncertain, pending autopsy results."

Bruce Smith. Dear, crazy Bruce Smith. I close my eyes and remember.

The seminary had placed me, for some kind of urban ministry practice setting, in a homeless shelter in the basement of a crumbling inner-city Methodist church. People were trapped down there in what I came to think of as Christianity's basement.

I was supposed to figure out what to do about the situation. Like a mad scientist turned loose in the asylum, I, a seminarian, was loosed on the spirits of thirty-some dirt-crusted human lives.

We held Sunday evening services. Broke bread, read the Bible, sang "How Great Thou Art" and other Elvis hits. Lit candles for the urban dead and mutilated, watched movies on the VCR until some-body stole it, played Bingo for cigarettes. I found myself begging these people to believe that God's love was broad and deep enough to include − without doubt − the unemployed, the unlucky, the un-washed.

Some dozed off. But a few, and among them Bruce Smith, began to change.

First he quit drinking. Then he got into arguing with me. Arguing, debating, theologizing, mostly about whether God cared. And then one night he came with an announcement. The basement was his raw material, his artist's pallet, he said. God's will for him was to create a theater company that would force the world to look at this basement. Expose its rankness to the fresh and holy air of artistic truth. And also, make some money.

Bruce Smith and I entered into a kind of partnership, or maybe it was a covenant. We sought power, he and I, power to execute his dream. To that end, I had things Bruce didn't have: like teeth, which impress people at funding interviews. And money connections, church connections.

He, on the other hand, had things I lacked: the ability to con a person out of their own skin. Humor. Stage presence. Street connec-tions.

We formed a chaotic theater company of basement dwellers. He directed. I managed. We rehearsed in the sun-filled sanctuary of First Church. Invited the public.

Opening night was hot, ninety-two degrees. We expected twenty-five, maybe thirty, people. Stuck an apple cider jar in the lobby for donations.

We'd vastly underestimated our power, Bruce Smith and I. Three-hundred-some people crammed the sanctuary that night. We hit the papers. Jobs poured in — a humanities commission, a TV show deal, school invitations, this, that, the other thing.

And in the peak of our unexpected fame, Bruce Smith ran away with the apple cider jug, well over five-hundred dollars, which plummeted him into his last drunk. The other actors found him later, beat him senseless — maybe even lifeless.

So Bruce Smith is dead now. The obituary says so. I whisper to him, across that mysterious divide between the living and the dead, "Hey, Bruce Smith, just because you're gone doesn't mean I like it or that I'll ever forget you or that people still have to live in basements. I hate basements. I was even there once. Under a train table. A long time ago . . .

"So I'll just go on without you, Mr. Disney Spielberg, and if you insist on being dead, I'll just build this ministry right on your back. No way will I let your life go to waste."

I can hear him saying, "Yea, yea, yea, okay. So. Stay on my back. Just do a better job this time, will you? Here's the thing. You gotta have power to change things, to create things. But, honey, you also gotta sit in a circle together and love each other. Gotta have both. I needed more than just making the show. I needed to argue with you more about God loving me. To sing 'How Great Thou Art' more. I needed, well to tell the truth, you coulda just held my hand more. Even if it was just a dirty basement.

"But, hey, not to worry. You got promise. As a minister, that is. So carry on, Miss Pearly Whites. Build yourself a ministry on my back. I can take it."

But I want the final word. So I whisper it. Softly. "You're right, Bruce Smith. Power and Love. The big show and the hand held. Always tight. Like a knot. That will be my ministry."

CHAPTER 32
NADINE

Nadine knew what it was like to go to the mountaintop. She'd been there herself. From there, she had found, you could see the silver thread that binds all peoples together.

Nadine had gone to the mountaintop a year after her husband had been killed by an anesthesiologist's mistake during minor surgery. Actually, her husband wasn't killed right away. He was in a coma for a year or so first, while Nadine took care of the kids, four of them, and worked.

And when he did die, then Nadine went to the mountaintop. She went in a dream.

First she got about halfway up and had a terrible fall that took her all the way back to the bottom. But then she started up again, even though she was exhausted. The closer she got to the top, the more exhausted she became, until she just plain couldn't get any further.

Right then, God's hand came down and pulled her up the rest of the way. So she also learned a thing or two about God, who seemed not a fatherly type with a beard, or a king in a heavenly kingdom, so much as a hand. A hand that would help you get to where you're going when you were just about done in.

When Nadine reached the mountaintop, God showed her the silver threads and told her to tend them. So she found out what she was supposed to be doing. It was up to her to form that into a calling.

And her calling, over the years, became helping people figure out how to buy homes. But not just any people. People who thought of themselves as too poor or undeserving to have homes. They would struggle into Nadine's little office, and her mission would begin anew.

Instead of saying, "How big is your paycheck now?" or, "Tell me about your credit rating," she would say with that smile of hers, "Now just exactly what sort of home do you want?"

And if they would respond with the word House, not Home, she'd gently correct them. Because Nadine didn't deal in houses, real estate, buildings, and grounds. She dealt in homes. Where the heart is. Where the silver threads become tangled to form a unique knot of love and kinship.

Sometimes they'd say, "Hey, who CARES what kind of home I'd like? For the money we've got, it don't matter."

But she would insist. Insist that they begin with what they wanted. It was her way of insisting that they acknowledge their dignity, their right to have wishes and dreams, no matter what the world seemed to be telling them.

And if she could get to them, which was almost always, they would risk a wish or two.

"Well, you know what, it would be a pleasure to have a front porch, the kind you sit on in summertime and watch the kids play." Or, "I've always wanted a fireplace, truth to tell." Or, "Wouldn't it be nice to get the baby into his own room?"

Upon these fragile dreams, Nadine would build a plan. Act as consultant, friend, interpreter, educator. No holding back. Use all her connections, her wiles, her skills, and her heart.

She would get them into places, their own places, Nadine would. Often against great odds. And if you asked how she did it, she'd just say, "Praise God!"

When they officially named Nadine's first loan project the "Hope" Program, she smiled, raised her brow like she does sometimes, and cast a little secret glance toward heaven. Without even knowing it, they'd done something special. For the name itself — Nadine — means "Hope."

EPILOGUE

THE WOMEN'S GROUP

The Women's Group will meet. At LaShella's house this time, and soon. Nadine, Marsha, Lydia, Deborah, all the others. We will sit in a circle exhausted, for it will be dusk and the end of a long day's work.

From some dusty back drawer, Laura will have brought out tea napkins with lovely pink border flowers, and these, with coffee and cookies, will be waiting for us. Will bring a certain eucharistic holiness to the fading of the light.

I will listen to the others with a full heart, for I have learned that silence is barren. That separateness is barren. That power without love is barren. That only the noisy, loving tangle of our combined voices, woven together by the very hand of God, can fashion a truth strong enough to sustain us and our peoples.

"I want to put a discussion of a Women's Retreat on the agenda." This from the determined Fay.

"Yes, and let's discuss who we want on the Executive Committee of the Neighborhood Group next year. After all, we women have a majority on the Board, and a vote is coming up." This from the persistent Laura.

"And before we begin, let us pray." This from the spirit-filled Nadine.

I can see. The baby will live. Our tiny beloved one, whom Pharaoh wants dead. We will, amidst God's sustaining presence, save this baby's life at the birthing stool. Making a basket of bitumen and pitch, we will kiss, launch, rescue, nurse, name, love this sweet infant into full potential. Feed it manna, even manna from a dumpster, if need be.

We will, through God's abiding love, hold our baby like a halo-haired child. Teach this beloved child to catch cockroaches, grow strong on Sunday Supper Enchilada Bake, draw with colored chalk upon excellent paper, and feel the powerful embrace of loving community.

We will birth the slow miracle of liberation. By God and through God and for God. We will keep hope alive.

This baby . . . this baby is going to live.

G. F. THOMPSON, a Unitarian Universalist minister, has for most of twenty years lived, labored, and celebrated life in America's urban core. Her ministry is woven from strands of experience in homeless shelters, programs for disturbed youth, immigrant organizations, and community organizing work in the areas of education, crime, housing, and women's rights.

Reverend Thompson presently shares in the ministry of a large urban church and maintains an ardent love of city life: noisy traffic, bright lights, bus rides, crowds, and — most of all — good hard fights for the sake of human dignity.

Other LuraMedia Publications

BANKSON, MARJORY ZOET

Braided Streams:
Esther and a Woman's Way of Growing

Seasons of Friendship:
Naomi and Ruth as a Pattern

"This Is My Body. . .":
Creativity, Clay, and Change

BORTON, JOAN

Drawing from the Women's Well: *Reflections on the Life Passage of Menopause*

CARTLEDGE-HAYES, MARY

To Love Delilah:
Claiming the Women of the Bible

DARIAN, SHEA

Seven Times the Sun:
Guiding Your Child through the Rhythms of the Day

DOHERTY, DOROTHY ALBRACHT and McNAMARA, MARY COLGAN

Out of the Skin Into the Soul:
The Art of Aging

DUERK, JUDITH

Circle of Stones:
Woman's Journey to Herself

I Sit Listening to the Wind:
Woman's Encounter within Herself

GOODSON, WILLIAM (with Dale J.)

Re-Souled: *Spiritual Awakenings of a Psychiatrist and his Patient in Alcohol Recovery*

HAGEN, JUNE STEFFENSEN, Editor

Rattling Those Dry Bones:
Women Changing the Church

JEVNE, RONNA FAY

It All Begins With Hope:
Patients, Caretakers, and the Bereaved Speak Out

The Voice of Hope:
Heard Across the Heart of Life

with ALEXANDER LEVITAN
No Time for Nonsense:
Getting Well Against the Odds

KEIFFER, ANN

Gift of the Dark Angel: *A Woman's Journey through Depression toward Wholeness*

LAIR, CYNTHIA

Feeding the Whole Family: *Down-to-Earth Cookbook and Whole Foods Guide*

LODER, TED

Eavesdropping on the Echoes:
Voices from the Old Testament

Guerrillas of Grace:
Prayers for the Battle

Tracks in the Straw:
Tales Spun from the Manger

Wrestling the Light:
Ache and Awe in the Human-Divine Struggle

MEYER, RICHARD C.

One Anothering: *Biblical Building Blocks for Small Groups*

MODJESKA, LEE

Keeper of the Night: *A Portrait of Life in the Shadow of Death*

NELSON, G. LYNN

Writing and Being: *Taking Back Our Lives through the Power of Language*

O'HALLORAN, SUSAN and DELATTRE, SUSAN

The Woman Who Lost Her Heart:
A Tale of Reawakening

PRICE, H.H.

Blackberry Season:
A Time to Mourn, A Time to Heal

RAFFA, JEAN BENEDICT

The Bridge to Wholeness:
A Feminine Alternative to the Hero Myth

Dream Theatres of the Soul:
Empowering the Feminine through Jungian Dreamwork

ROTHLUEBBER, FRANCIS

Nobody Owns Me: *A Celibate Woman Discovers her Sexual Power*

RUPP, JOYCE

The Star in My Heart:
Experiencing Sophia, Inner Wisdom

THOMPSON, G. F.

Slow Miracles: *Urban Women Fighting for Liberation*

WEEMS, RENITA J.

I Asked for Intimacy: *Stories of Blessings, Betrayals, and Birthings*

Just a Sister Away: *A Womanist Vision of Women's Relationships in the Bible*

LuraMedia, Inc.
7060 Miramar Rd., Suite 104
San Diego, CA 92121

Books for Healing and Hope,
Balance and Justice
Call 1-800-FOR-LURA for information.